RICHARD BRAMWELL

Signs of Life

Richard Bramwell

First published in 2017
by Richard Bramwell
www.richardbramwell.me.uk

ISBN 978-1-9998950-0-6

Richard Bramwell was born in Sheffield.
He now lives in north-west England with his
wife, Eileen.

"I owe much to my parents. One of my
earliest memories is listening to my mother
recite poems. She instilled in me a love of
language. She encouraged me to read and to
listen, to look and learn. She inspired me
to face life, day by day, whatever worries or
wonders it may bring."

To Eileen

Contents

Childhood Home

And there it stands, the fortress tall,
Surrounded by a mighty wall;
When I was young it looked so high
It seemed to blot out half the sky.
I see, with an embarrassed smile,
I have outgrown it by a mile.

Beyond the ramparts lies the home,
The house that was a home to me.
This was the place where I began,
Transformed through childhood into man.
Who lives there now, they're not my kin;
I'm on the outside, looking in.

Some sounds and scenes invade my head:
I'm lying, tucked up in my bed,
Wake up, see shadows on the wall,
Listen to footsteps in the hall;
The smell of bacon wafts my way –
Better than cabbage any day.

Indoors there's not much privacy
Outside is where I like to be.
The garden still looks overgrown;
One hiding place was all my own,
I hid all night once, for a dare,
And no-one ever found me there.

Though tears are streaming down my face
I have no claim upon this place.
Hold out my hand, and touch the air:
The walls stay silent, without care;
I turn, and slowly walk away.
The orphanage was yesterday.

Binary Code

The hours that anxious parents wait
For those first words their baby utters,
Cajoling, willing you to speak
Then "Quiet, it's rude to interrupt."

The stories doting parents tell
Of tooth fairies and Santa Claus.
But what do they say later on?
"It's wrong to tell fibs, don't tell tales."

When Mr Punch hits crocodiles
The adults laugh, it's funny,
But when you play and hit the dog
They scowl and say it's cruel.

"Eat up, don't waste your food
It makes you big and strong."
But later, hungry, growing up,
"Don't over-eat, it's wrong."

"Take exercise, you should get out,
Not stay in staring at a screen."
Your parents nag you endlessly
But take you in a car to school.

"Don't be selfish, share your toys."
But they are none too pleased
When you share answers to the tests
With others in the class.

Is it any wonder?

Spirit of Learning

I first discovered words and books
when I was only four.
As more years passed my body grew
but it could only run so fast.
My mind could fly,
moved by stories beyond my dreams.
I was elemental.
I could go anywhere, do anything, in my head –
until mum came, said "Lights out, time for bed".

I played football, was picked for the team.
I learned the language of the game,
to curve the ball and when to fall,
in fair weather and foul.

I wanted wheels, I wanted speed.
I learned to drive, acquired the skill,
learned the rules, the driveway code,
in combat with machines that kill.

I joined the army, why not?
Endured the training and the drill.
Learned the sights, felt the thrill.
Was sent on active service.
Our platoon leader was all-active man.
I was inspired, and soon breathed my last.

Introductions

Flattered, the fly met the windscreen,
Playful, the mouse met the cat,
Fulfilled, the tooth met the dentist,
And bashful, the ball met the bat.

Light-headed, the moth met the flame,
Red-faced, the leaf met the ground,
Sweetly, the bloom met the bee,
And gamely, the fox met the hound.

Enchanted, the song met the fans,
Expectant, the bride met the groom
Delighted, the fire met the hose,
And crossly, the weft met the loom.

Uplifted, the worm met the bird,
Alluring, the fish met the hook,
Big-headed, the beer met the glass,
And bemused, the words met the book.

Encounters

When people meet for the first time
Our ancient instincts take control,
To size the other person up,
To classify, to pigeon-hole.

Our first impressions count a lot,
Evaluating looks and face;
In this our eyes do all the work,
Expanding our mind's database.

And if we then have time to speak
The situation may grow tense:
Our questions relay mental probes
To gather more intelligence.

"Do you have any children, then?"
They ask it without emphasis.
So simple, so innocuous,
Yet such a loaded question, this.

If childless you are selfish, odd,
Not one of them, you don't belong.
Their box is ticked, your place assigned,
Unthinking that they may be wrong.

face beat

diane lives in the flat above
i feel it when shes on the move
we hug and walk off down the street
were going to the club tonight

its always crowded in the place
its hard to talk to get some space
the lights flash twice and then turn low
its time to go and watch the show
we find some seats a table too

the first acts funny tells us jokes
i know that one the two old blokes
then music starts up fast and bright
dianes on stage her face in lights
her lips are moving to the beat
i feel it through the wooden floor
the feelings good i grin for more
we wave our hands up in the air
we stay and sway the vibes are great
with beat and rhythm i am hot
i thump the table look at me
another drink my turn to buy
she comes and joins us looking great
i tell her she is good tonight

the club doors close we linger on
dont lose your bag you put it down
a final wave we go back home
some peace at last now im alone

Now Man
To H.M.

Hello, I'm Henry, who are you?
I know I'm here, some where, some place.
The same old things are always new.

Some how, the view has gone askew.
I have no label for the space.
Hello, I'm Henry, who are you?

I see no sign, no guide, no clue.
I know a clock but not a face.
The same old things are always new.

I never did but what I do.
I know a word but not the case.
Hello, I'm Henry, who are you?

I think, but can't find what I knew.
Today I have no database.
The same old things are always new.

My life's a maze I wander through.
When I look back, I see no trace.
Hello, I'm Henry, who are you?
The same old things are always new.

Henry Molaison had surgery in 1953, aged 27, hoping to cure
debilitating epilepsy. Part of his brain was removed and he was
left with no ability to store or retrieve new experiences. For the
next 55 years, Henry lived in the permanent present moment.

Fuming Mad

The car sat, fuming.
Gulping petrol, choked with air.
Spitting out particulates.

The man sat, fuming.
He was the driver.
He was going places.
He was.

Nose to tail.
Bumper to boot.
White light to red.

Traffic snarled.
People cursed.
Headlights glared.
Tempers flared.
Tailback grew.

The car sat, fuming.

The Roadside Verge

Along the verge, set in the grass,
Are multi-coloured flowers en masse.
I put on my glasses
And now I see masses
Of crisp packets, beer cans and glass.

The Roadside Shrine

There once was a bridge down a hill
Where nothing much happened, until
A car came too fast,
Drove over, not past;
Now flowers recall the last thrill.

Time Off

We spend one third of all our lives
While body rests and mind revives
Asleep.

We twitch and dream, we toss and turn
But don't achieve, don't work or earn
Asleep.

Is our existence frivolous?
To meaning we're oblivious
Asleep.

In company or all alone
We live life in the slumberzone
Asleep.

Sound Asleep

Giraffes will do it standing up
Whilst bats are happy upside down;
Fish do it as they drift along,
But astronauts must be tied down.

We humans are most versatile
And do it front or back or side,
(Though prehistoric fears dictate
We do it in the dark, and hide).

Some creatures do lots more than us –
Koalas do most of the day;
Some animals just hibernate
To while the winter months away.

For humans hoping for sweet dreams
There is one soporific flaw:
As people worldwide still complain,
Why do their partners have to snore?

Having a Check-up

A member of the medical profession
has diagnosed a case of mild obsession
and while he is well-known for his discretion
in order to avoid yet more repression
I feel that I must make a small confession:
the note in which his judgment finds expression
is now, I cannot lie, in my possession.

I suffer from a very slight fixation,
I have to double-check, it's my vocation;
the treatment he prescribed as my salvation
to rid me of this troubling aberration
he gave me there and then, no hesitation:
and to ensure my total liberation
I've been and booked a second consultation.

Lifestyles

Worried well. Use a gel.

Feel unwell. What the hell.

Self-obsessed. Take a test.

Over-stressed. More depressed.

Pay the bill. Overkill.

Pop a pill. Go downhill.

Try cocaine. Find a vein.

Suffer pain. Can't complain.

Land Girl, 1917

'Dig ditches for the King and countryside',
'Follow the plough', we swallowed all that guff;
The girls are coming, old men stand aside.

I volunteered, I made my mark with pride –
Some said it wasn't right, the work too tough:
Dig ditches for the King and countryside.

Who knew what we could do until we tried?
Some days knee-deep in ditches, mud and stuff,
The girls are coming, old men stand aside.

They came and told me my man Tom had died.
An afternoon it was, I took it rough.
Dig ditches for the King and countryside.

I stood beside the gate and shook and cried,
And then I ploughed the top field, straight enough.
The girls are coming, old men stand aside.

A widow now, and not four years a bride –
The mattock's edge was rusty, it was duff.
Dig ditches for the King and boys who died:
The girls are coming, old men stand aside.

The Women's Land Army was formed during the
First World War.

The Brick

"Will they remember me in years to come?
A hundred years from now, will people care?
I did not think I would be brave enough,
But here, today, I feel I will, I dare:

It's so unfair, the state in which we live.
My husband and the courts say it's a crime
To dare to question what they say is right;
I only know, within myself, it's time.

One final task before I leave the house –
I wrap myself within a cloak of grey.
Across my dress, the green and purple sash
Lies gently waiting for the light of day.

I'm not alone, but do not know her name:
So rosy-cheeked, she looks a country lass.
Abandoning my guise, I loose my cloak.
I pick the brick, and hurl it through the glass."

I close the book, with one eye on the clock,
Put on one side the diary that she wrote.
With practised thumbs I choose and click to send:
He looks and sings the best, he gets my vote.

Two Sides of the Coin

I

Des Kingsley knew he'd earned his wealth.
He'd built his business up from scratch,
from sorting scrap to smelting plant,
created with hard work and sweat
and profits that outstripped his debt.

He'd not had help from silver spoon –
but hoped to be 'Sir Desmond' soon.
A big employer in the town,
he sponsored local groups and teams
and so was held in high esteem.

He never minded being seen
in his expensive limousine.
Today, he wanted some cigars.
He drove himself and, to save time,
he parked on double yellow lines.

II

An anxious Danny scanned the street;
the call from Jen was bittersweet:
he knew he needed wheels at once.
He watched the gent parking his car
and thought he'd left the door ajar.

As casually as he knew how,
he sauntered over and he saw
the fool had left the keys as well.
He blessed the luck that came his way,
started the car and drove away.

His partner Jen was so relieved,
she hadn't let herself believe
that he would get to her so fast.
Her waters broke just after nine;
she knew they didn't have much time.

III

As Scott approached the hospital
he heard the car screech to a halt
and watched the couple stumble out.
While he admired its gleaming chrome,
he felt his foot tread on a stone:

it was a wallet on the ground.
Scott gave a rapid glance around
and pocketed the notes inside.
His brother Joe was in ward four,
along the cancer corridor.

Joe went to Kingsley's straight from school
and slowly had become unwell;
his lungs, that's what the doctors said.
Six months, a year? they didn't know.
Scott thought of ways to use the dough.

Second Sight

When we look in a mirror, what do we see?
Do we see ourselves, or who we'd like to be?

The characters reflecting back,
Who beam to meet our gaze,
Are they already in the past,
A littering of rays?

When I look in a mirror, who do I see?
Me looking at you, or you regarding me?

The person staring out at me,
Is it my father or my mother?
The portrait that half fills the glass,
Is this my self or someone other?

Can you see through the surface gloss,
Behind my glazed self-storage screen?
Where do you end and I begin;
Do we live somewhere in-between?

Hold a mirror to a face, see if it mists:
The spirit's condensation shows it exists.

An avatar of who we are,
A solid crystal hologram
That moves and poses in the light
Identical, but not the same.

To a Fault

Life's not been easy, no it's not.
Hardship, laughing, scrimping, pain.
I went to school some days, some not.
I dreamt the sunshine, got the rain.

Couldn't find work, did what I could.
Sometimes I'd earn, a pound or two.
One day I met him, standing there;
I felt him change me, through and through

I thought the sun shone out of him
But when a son came out of me
He upped and left, no second thought
He took the clothes and stuff we bought.

Life's not been easy, no it's not.
Hardship, crying, scrimping, pain.
I'm down to just one piece of bread.
I'll cut it, then we'll each have some.

War Game

The struggle soon intensified.
The hawks proposed all-out attack
Whilst doves, more wary of the foe,
Were all for caution, holding back.

The skirmish had become a war.
The target zone was in no doubt,
Not yet acquired, but clearly flagged,
Head-up displays had marked it out.

From recces of the key terrain
Intel identified the threats;
The risks were quantified, like odds
For poker players placing bets.

How many chips should he commit?
The cautious route went to one side,
It would encounter rougher ground
But forest offered place to hide.

Code Eagle was the direct route
To mobilise a swift assault,
It also carried higher risk
And this might be a fatal fault.

The hostiles were well-bunkered in.
His force could cope well over land
But they would need to cross a lake
And might well come to grief in sand.

The time had come to make a choice –
Attacking now, or not at all:
He shook his head, to clear his mind,
Then swung his club and struck the ball.

The Stage Door

Sebastian knew he was the star;
a prima donna, some would say.
A doyen of the repertoire,
he took the lead in every play.

He knew each script, if not by heart,
enough for him to play the role.
He loved the limelight and his art
and relished every scene he stole.

His speeches were often extended,
the cast were upstaged and surprised;
whatever directors intended,
he claimed he had extemporized.

He fluffed his lines and missed his cues,
he never played it by the book,
and yet he got the best reviews:
he had the presence and the look.

His fans applauded and they cheered
from both the circles and the stalls
each time their leading man appeared.
He always got more curtain calls.

One evening, he faltered mid-section
(the ASM swore he was yawning).
Unprompted, and losing direction,
his grand exit came without warning:

the trapdoor was open, stage right –
and 'someone' had turned out the light . . .

The Holiday

We've booked for a fortnight in Spain,
Full-board, and we're going by plane.
Then ash fills the sky
And no-one can fly
So back to the brochures again.

Look here, do you fancy a cruise?
Fine dining, and lots to amuse:
But out on the ocean,
That up and down motion –
It's not a vacation I'd choose.

A journey by train, that sounds fine
But no, with regret, we decline:
It's autumn, not spring,
And that means one thing –
The wrong sort of leaves on the line.

A coach tour, now what could go wrong?
We'll have fun, just bowling along;
But if there's no loo
Then what would I do?
I can't keep my legs crossed for long.

Well, after so much aggravation,
We're having a small celebration:
We both agree now
The where and the how –
We've settled on our destination.

So here I am, writing a card:
Our journey, well that wasn't hard;
The view is quite nice,
Home cooking – no spice –
There's nowhere quite like our back yard.

Villa Knell

We've emigrated here to sunny Spain:
This is our fifth successive month of drought.
Our lives will never be the same again.

Relax, soak up the sun and entertain –
We didn't know our agent was a tout.
We've emigrated here to sunny Spain:

The water from our pool's gone down the drain –
I wish we'd never heard of porous grout.
Our lives will never be the same again.

It would be good to see a drop of rain
But then, our concrete walls are not so stout.
We've emigrated here to sunny Spain:

The papers that we signed did not explain
How many building rules there were to flout.
Our lives will never be the same again.

The taxes that we owe give me a pain,
We can't afford to stay, but can't get out.
We've emigrated here to sunny Spain:
Our lives will never be the same again.

Welcome to Visitors from Overseas

Before they cross over the ocean
Do visitors have any notion,
A sense of the place,
Of this island race,
Of what sets this nation in motion?

Our weather can't fail to impress;
This morning, just how should I dress?
For sunshine or rain?
Or drizzle, again?
The best thing to do is to guess.

A thing that we British still do
Is forming an orderly queue:
Come rain or come shine
We wait in a line . . .
At sale times, a scrummage will do.

Our great British food may surprise –
It's more than just puddings and pies:
From east and from west
We've picked out the best,
From curries to burgers with fries.

And, if you should fancy a drink,
The choice here is more than you think:
You won't find us whingeing
As we go out bingeing,
We'll down a good glass in one blink.

Our great love of sport and fair play
Has entered the language today;
We say 'It's not cricket'
Or 'that sticky wicket'
And winning's not cool (just the pay).

The visitor out and about
Need not have a moment of doubt:
Throw phrase-book away
And go on your way,
As English is spoken throughout.

So, welcome to these British Isles –
Where distance is measured in miles –
We can't promise sun
(Or when trains will run)
But hope you'll meet plenty of smiles!

Table Talk

"Did you have a good day today?"
she asked as she paused in mid eat.
"So so," came his grunted reply,
"this morning we had that big meet.

The big boss lectured all of us
to 'pull together as a team'
when all we really want some days
is somewhere we can let off steam.

Restocking shelves is what I do,
I fill in gaps, I make up piles.
Should I talk team-work to the tins
then stack 'em up and watch their smiles?

But what about your own day, luv?
At least you're your own boss down there."
"Yeah, me an' Trace, she's good at nails
but hopeless when it comes to hair.

Old Mrs Barker missed her last,
she came in showing all her roots.
And Jess – you know, from Pilling Drive –
she's got a pair of those new boots – "

"Don't have the peas if they're not right,
they're way beyond their sell-by-date."
"They taste OK. But tell you what
I learned from Cath at number 8,

the two that live next door to her –
they dress like Goths, you know the pair –
we thought them heading for divorce,
turns out it's only an affair

not even married, and two kids.
She's thrown him out, he won't come back.
And if I save up all my tips
I could afford a pair in black.

Thing is, some days, my back does ache,
it's standing too long on my feet.
I know you do, but not stood still,
I'm glad to sit down when we eat."

She looked up from her dinner plate.
"I can't reach, can you pass the sauce?"
She pressed her thumb, he did the same,
ended the call and passed the sauce.

The Leaf; or, Autumn Happens

There once was a young leaf, named Bud,
Who unfurled as soon as he could.
He loved the sun's rays
On hot summer days
For sun-bathing made him feel good.

One morning, on his coat of green,
He noticed a sort of a sheen:
His friends called it 'rain'
And Bud, being vain,
Would use it to keep himself clean.

But one day as he glanced around
Some patches and blotches he found;
All yellow and brown,
He started to frown –
And fluttered his way to the ground.

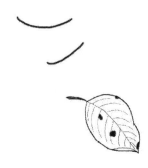

New Arrival (1)

Our first child, so tender, so small,
Holds both of us tight in his thrall.
Then night after night
Awake with the mite
Our rapture is starting to pall.

New Arrival (2)

For weeks we've been feeling quite strained,
At times our expression's been pained
But now, Oh what bliss!
No more hit and miss:
Our darling is now potty-trained.

Ongoing

The notion that creatures evolve
Gives rise to more puzzles to solve:
If microbes and man
Aren't part of some plan,
Then what does the process involve?

Nature or Nurture?

There once was a very small seed
That wondered how best to proceed:
It pondered a while –
Without any guile –
Should it become flower or weed?

Star Struck

How do we know that stars exist?
"The stars come out at night" you say
But where's your evidence, your proof?
Where are the stars by light of day?

Throughout the drama of mankind
The stars have always played a part,
Imbued with myths or life-forms strange
Or for some necromancer's art.

The homes of aliens or gods,
Or globes of incandescent gas?
All painted inside crystal spheres,
Or hung on model arms of brass?

Astronomers with awe observed
The speckled hem of heaven's drape,
Detected patterns in the stars
Gave names and portents to each shape.

Astrologers conspired with kings
Divined their fortunes, good or ill,
Persuading lords that their misrule
Was forced by fate and not by will.

Do stars exist apart from us
With all their age-long fascination,
Or are they products of the mind,
Pinpricks in our imagination?

Has anybody heard a star?
One single, solitary peep?
As birdsong chorus welcomes dawn
Do stellar singers herald sleep?

Do people gather on the hills
To listen to the twinkling sounds?
To catch the moonlit murmurings
Of stars in their nocturnal rounds.

Or have you ever met a man
Who's tasted stars and still is sane?
As if they're like some tender fruits
That ripen when the sunbeams wane.

Imagine what their flavours are
A spangled, sparkling, tingling taste
Well mingled in some cosmic sauce
Adding light-years to heaven's waist.

"Reach for the stars" is poor advice:
Beyond our grasp, try as we may:
All we can touch is emptiness,
They simply are so far away.

Are stars all soft, like gosling's down
Or burning, like a candle's flame;
Beneath their surface, thick with dust,
Is each unique, or all the same?

And no, we cannot smell the stars:
As daylight fades away to dusk
We don't exclaim in ecstasy
How sweet the scent of starry musk.

And yet, you say, there is a way,
Although we may not smell or feel:
The gift of light, our sense of sight,
This shows us that the stars are real.

But pause a moment and reflect –
The distances of space are vast:
Starlight that reaches us today
Shows only scenes from distant past;

Our present sky might all be dark:
The stars we thought we saw about,
Like sparks cast by the primal forge,
Have dimmed, and flickered, and gone out.

This could explain our childhood's dread
To go to sleep without a light;
If needed, here's a comforter
To keep you safe at dead of night:

Approach the teller of this tale
With open hand (no need of fist)
And tap them smartly on the head.
They then will know that stars exist.

Internet

The web's an amazing creation
It gives me so much information
I sit at the screen
And, while my mind's keen,
My body has lost all sensation.

New-weather-speak

Those flakes that you see, they're not snow
We've got global warming, you know
It's sunlight in slivers
That's giving you shivers –
And watch for hot ice as you go!

The Sad Prince

There once was a greeny-brown frog
Who thought, as he sat on a log,
Of all he did miss,
Awaiting one kiss –
For more, you must go to his blog.

Current Affairs

Witness an incident
~~A tragic shame, learn why and how~~
Who's to blame, indict someone now

Take part in sport
~~Strive and compete~~
Take drugs and cheat

Go for a drive
~~Follow road signs, find the way~~
Follow satnavs, go astray

Make a blunder
~~Use common sense~~
Take offence

Describe an event
~~Tell the whole truth, give balanced views~~
Text the troll truth, invent fake news

Express true love
~~Whisper sweet nothings~~
Text and tweet nothings

Discuss an issue
~~Have a reasoned debate~~
Use invective of hate

Hear different opinions
~~Show a brave face~~
Find a safe place

Produce a report
~~Use balanced writing~~
Come out fighting

Announce a meeting tomorrow
~~Give today's news~~
Speculate views

Meet someone famous
~~Be on cloud nine~~
Post selfies on-line

Reg'lations

"On bonfires, place nothing too high;
Wear headgear, and cover each eye;
Protect hands and feet
Against excess heat" –
And those are the rules for the guy.

Real Life

When I went to buy a new hat
The sales person said to me that
The price would be less
If I would say yes
And take it home with me packed flat.

Transparency

A goldfish went round in his bowl,
He was an adventurous soul:
For just on a whim
He'd pause in mid-swim
And blow bubbles up at the hole.

Natural Rhythm

"Come dancing," he said, "it's not hard."
And so I let Bill mark my card.
Instead of a ball
We had a great fall –
He'd rumba'd as I cha-cha-cha'd.

Companions

There was a young girl named Simone
Who went everywhere with her phone:
While out for a walk
She'd text and she'd talk,
Not lonely – but always alone.

Underheard

He looks at me like I'm absurd,
Not knowing his hearing is blurred.
I say "I'm a poet"
And, wouldn't you know it,
He thinks I'm a parrot, a bird.

Going Metric

"Your verse," said the purist, "won't rhyme."
And I said, "I just don't have time
To check every word,
So don't be absurd –
And surely, it's not an offence?"

Dotage

I saw them on my arms and hands –
Pale freckles scattered on the skin:
I wasn't worried what they were,
Just cells with extra melanin.

I had them when I was a child
In summer, in the holiday,
And when I started back at school
They faded and they went away.

I felt a bit self-conscious then,
And getting teased was not much fun,
But I grew up, and learned the cause
Was being outdoors, in the sun.

This morning wasn't quite the same.
It was a shock, I must admit:
The mirror showed them on the face
That stared back when I looked at it.

They say our skin renews itself,
Dead cells are shed and new ones grow –
So how could freckles have survived
For longer than a month or so?

Bright sunny days have been and gone,
It isn't summer any more
But dull and grey November time;
My freckles had all gone before.

The blotches that I notice now
Are spots of age, and will not fade.
Unlike the sun-spots of my youth
They grow indoors and in the shade.

Now I've been branded, marked for life,
And bear the signs for all to know:
My body's lasted three-score years
But may not have much more to go.

Born to Greatness

My doctor said, "Please lose some weight,
At twelve stones your bulk is too great."
That new liquid diet,
I thought I would try it –
And now I'm one over the eight .

.

.

Dawning

Time's pesky barbs have found their mark,
My hair is grey that once was dark;
My teeth aren't all real,
One hip is half steel –
So why do I wake with the lark?

In the Care Home Lounge

We've come to the end of the line;
Old age has robbed life of its shine.
We sit here all day,
As time ebbs away –
Who's that in the chair next to mine?

Hospital Corridor

The corridor, echoing, bright
With smells that just fail to delight:
A man gives a yawn,
His new son is born
And sobs mark a soul put to flight.

"A Merry Christmas ..."
"Bah!" said Scrooge, "Humbug!"

Jingle tills, jingle tills,
Jingle every day
From August to December
Retailing Christmas Day.

Swipe and tap, scan and beep,
Pinging all the way,
Oh! what fun it is to shop . . .
Until it's time to pay.

Sparkling lights, flashing lights,
Twinkle in the air,
Blinging malls and bustling streets
Flogging gifts and festive fare.

Tingle nose, tingle toes,
Frozen snow and slush,
Market huts, roast chestnuts,
Jostle through the crush.

Dazzled nights, frazzled days,
Partying all the way,
Stuffed with food, sloshed with booze,
Bingeing life away.

Tempers frayed, bills unpaid,
Up to here with Christmas cheer,
Turkey stuffed, table laid,
Thank God it's only once a year.

P.S.

I enclose the receipt
If this verse doesn't fit.

82487749R00030

Made in the USA
Columbia, SC
17 December 2017